CONTENTS

KT-363-860

SNOWBOARDING

Pro rider Chris Moran pushes snowboarding to a new level on the amazing slopes of East Greenland. Temperature: down to –65˚C!

OVERVIEW

Snowboarding is a fun, healthy and thrilling sport. It's like skateboarding and surfing, but it is done on snowy mountains. Zooming down the slopes, snowboarders feel very free.

SNOWBOARDING

Snowboarders must travel to the mountains to get to the snow.

If you want to learn to snowboard, you can take lessons. Or, your snowboarding friends can teach you.

HISTORY

The first snowboard was invented almost a hundred years ago. The early snowboards were like stand-up sledges and hard to ride. They did not even have bindings!

Here are some of the first snowboards.

The first snowboard sold was called The Snurfer.

Two Americans called Tom Sims and Jake Burton Carpenter made snowboarding trendy in the 1970s. They set up snowboarding companies.

Tom Sims (far right) and Jake Burton Carpenter (far left) in 1983

*The monoski came before
the snowboard.*

**A French ski instructor called Régis Rolland
made Europe's first snowboarding film.
It was called *Apocalypse Snow*. It was
made in 1983.**

Today, snowboarding is the world's most
popular winter sport. There are nearly
14 million riders around the world.

A scene from
Apocalypse Snow

*An early snowboard
being built.*

Apocalypse Snow

Three *Apocalypse
Snow* films were
made. The costumes
were colourful and
the stunts incredible.
The films are still
popular today.

TYPES OF SNOWBOARDING

Freeriding

Freeriding is when you use the whole mountain as a playground. Usually snowboarders use trails that are specially marked out.

Freeriders like to ride in deep powder snow. They like to ride the steepest parts of the mountain. They even jump off cliffs!

SNOWBOARDING

A half pipe

Freestyle

Freestyle snowboarders copy skateboarding and surfing tricks.

Jibbing

This type of snowboarding copies the moves of urban skateboarders on the street.

Snowboarders ride on obstacles such as rails.

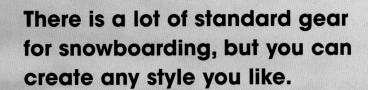

There is a lot of standard gear for snowboarding, but you can create any style you like.

DIFFERENT BOARDS

Without snow, there would be no snowboarding! Riders need to protect themselves from the cold and snow and the many different weather conditions found in the mountains.

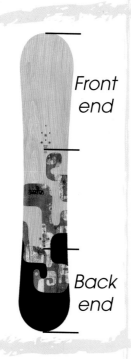

Front
end

Back
end

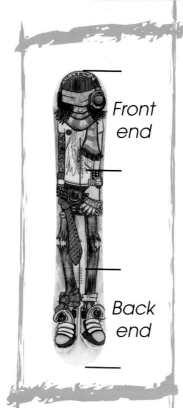

Front
end

Back
end

Front
end

Back
end

Freeride board

Freeride boards are wide so that they can 'float' better on top of deep snow. They are longer at the front than the back.

Freestyle board

Freestyle boards are light, short and have a nose and tail of the same length. You can ride the board backwards and forwards, jump and spin.

Powder board

Powder boards are very long. They are designed to be ridden as quickly as possible, in steep and deep snow. If the board has a short or light tail, the rider's weight is at the back of it.

DESIGN

Deck   Base

Deck and base

The top of the snowboard is the deck. This is where the rider's feet are strapped in.

The part in contact with the snow is called the base.

Metal edges

The most important parts of the board are the sharp metal edges.

They help the board to turn by cutting into the snow.

Bindings

The metal and plastic bindings are very stiff. They attach the rider to the board by their feet.

WHAT TO WEAR

Snowboarders must wear the right clothing for protection. The gear shields them from the sun and snow and protects their body from falls.

Boots

Boots give support and protection. They fit the bindings of the board.

Gloves

Snow gloves are hard-wearing, waterproof and cosy inside.

Helmet

Helmets protect the head. Wearing one could save your life.

Goggles

Goggles protect your eyes from snow-spray and bright sunlight.

CRAZY FASHION

Although it is important for the clothing to protect the rider, it doesn't mean it can't also look good.

The 1980s

In the 1980s, snow fashion was influenced by the bright neon colours of the surf world.

The 1990s

By the 1990s, skateboarding and hip hop became more important influences. Riders wore baggy clothes and had dreadlocks.

Today

These days, snowboarding fashion is about being an individual.

THE MOUNTAIN

SNOWBOARDING

With peaks of 4,809 metres and snowfall all year round, the French Alps are one of the most popular winter-sports destinations.

RESORTS OF THE WORLD

Central Europe

Countries in the European Alpine area, such as Austria, France and Italy, are popular with snowboarders.

Europe was where the world speed snowboarding record was set.

French Alps

SNOWBOARDING

Breckenridge, Colorado

USA

America is the home of snowboarding. It has some of the world's most famous riders, biggest slopes, best pipes and trickiest jumps.

Mount Tasman

New Zealand

When it is summer in the northern hemisphere, many snowboarders head to New Zealand. It has some of the steepest cliffs and biggest drops.

TYPES OF TERRAIN

Piste

Pistes/Trails

These are the routes where most skiers and snowboarders can be found in a ski resort. They get groomed each night by huge machines called piste bashers.

SNOWBOARDING

Off-piste

Off-piste is every part of the in-resort area that isn't a piste!

Off-piste sections are playgrounds of fresh snow, but they can be dangerous.

Backcountry

The backcountry is the mountain wilderness outside a resort's boundaries.

It is appealing for many riders, but there can be avalanches and unpredictable weather.

SNOW BUSINESS

The weather in the mountains can change very quickly. Here are some facts and figures about snow.

Temperature

As long as there is moisture in the air and a way for it to rise and form clouds, there can be snow – even in temperatures below zero.

Blizzards

As soon as the temperature hits less than –7°C with winds greater than 55km/h, heavy snowfall is considered a blizzard. Visibility is reduced.

Fresh powder

Most heavy snowfalls occur above –9°C.

Types of snow

Snow is different around the world. This is because individual snow crystals contain different amounts of liquid.

Drier snow is called 'powder'. The board glides faster, and turns become spectacular in fresh powder.

Blizzards are extremely destructive and dangerous.

UNUSUAL RESORTS

Iran

Iran might not be the most obvious place to go snowboarding. However, the resorts of Dizin and Shemshak have great snow, empty slopes, friendly locals and fantastic food.

Atlas mountains

Morocco

Morocco is one of the only places in the world where you can go surfing in the sea one day and snowboarding the next.

Where next?

Exotic places like Greenland, Russia and even Antarctica have been explored by riders looking for the next best thing.

Greenland

MOUNTAIN SAFETY

An avalanche is a very large and sudden rush of snow down a mountain. When snowboarding off-piste always carry the following kit.

Transceiver

Sometimes known as a 'beeper', this is a rider's lifeline. It gives out a signal so that a trapped person can be found.

SNOWBOARDING

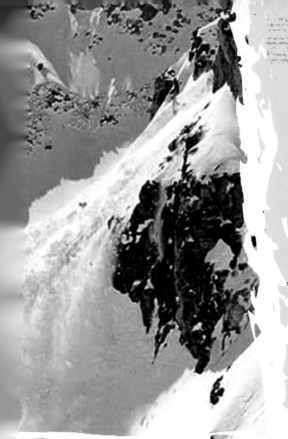

This is world freeriding champion Craig Kelly. He was killed by an avalanche.

Backpack

Riders carry a backpack to store their shovel, probe and other essentials such as food and a medical kit.

Shovel

Shovels are used to dig out victims.

Probe

A probe is a fold-away marker that is placed in the snow above the buried victim. This pinpoints their position.

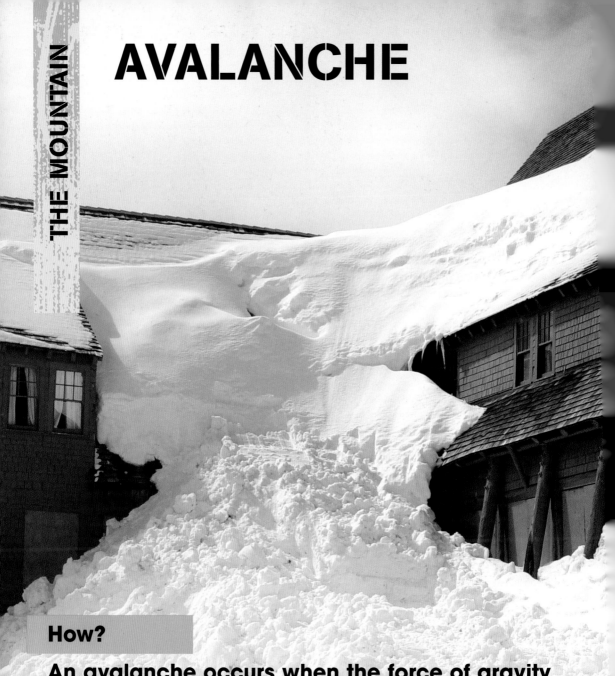

AVALANCHE

How?

An avalanche occurs when the force of gravity trying to pull the snow downhill is greater than the strength of the bonds between the layers of snow.

A trigger is needed to set the snow sliding. This could be the weight of a snowboarder.

SNOWBOARDING

When?

Most avalanches occur in January, February and March when the snowfall is heaviest.

Some avalanches occur in April when the snow is thawing.

Rescuers use a probe and shovel to locate a victim.

A powder avalanche

Where?

Most avalanches start on slopes of between 30 and 45 degrees.

Most skiing and snowboarding slopes are between 25 and 50 degrees.

CHAPTER 4: TRICKS AND STUNTS

Japanese rider Sinsuke Saitou performs an Indie grab at a height of four metres in the air.

JUMPS

For most riders, snowboarding is all about leaving the ground!

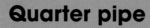

Quarter pipe

Riders aim at the steep wall of the quarter pipe. They are shot high into the air. Then they land on the same wall. They perform tricks high in the air.

SNOWBOARDING

Fun parks

Fun parks look like skateboarding parks.

The parks have jumps and obstacles such as handrails and even picnic benches!

Half pipe

Riders use a half pipe to reach for the skies. They perform difficult tricks when they are in the air.

This photo shows Quentin Robbins from New Zealand. He is a champion snowboarder.

Half pipe

HANDRAILS

Jibbing started as an underground movement. Today, it is a big business.

Fifteen years ago, freestyle was popular, but the pipes were poor and jumps were small. Jibbing opened up a new area to explore.

Jeremy Jones

By the mid 90s, jibbing had died out. Then a group of riders from Salt Lake City in America reignited the flame.

Jibbers practise tricks that they then perform on snow or in urban areas. Some jibbers just ride rails!

Jake Blauvelt

TRICKS

A trick is anything that involves leaving the ground or using an obstacle to perform a stunt. Whoever makes up the trick gets to pick the name. There are some very odd trick names.

British pro Adam Gendle performs the Indie grab

Grabs

Grabs are taken from skateboarding tricks. You can make up new tricks by grabbing the board in different places.

Method

The Method grab is difficult. Grab the heel edge of the board between your feet with your front hand. Then push your back leg out.

Indie

This is the easiest grab. Grab the board between your toes with your back hand.

Roast beef

Grab the toe edge of the board with your back hand after having put it through your legs from the back. Sounds tricky – and it is!

HARDEST TRICKS

Since the beginning, riders have been trying to outdo each other with their hardest spins. A '360' means one complete rotation in the air.

The McTwist is an upside-down 540-degree rotation. The rider does 1.5 spins in mid-air before touching down on the snow again.

Terje Håkonsen performing a McTwist.

A frontside 360

Finnish rider Markku Koski landed the first-ever backwards 1440 (four full rotations). He did this at the 2002 US Open.

Markku Koski performing a 1440.

In 2008, German pro David Benedek was captured on film doing a trick called a 'double-corked 1080' – three full rotations spun like a corkscrew!

World-famous US gold medallist
Hannah Teter performs in the half pipe
at the 2006 Winter Olympics in Turin, Italy.

TOP CONTESTS

Snowboarding is a very exciting sport to watch. There are many national and international contests around the world.

SNOWBOARDING

Travice Rice on his way to winning the Air and Style 2006.

Air and Style

The Air and Style is held in the Olympic stadium in Munich, Germany. The world's best freestyle riders compete on huge ramps.

Sponsorship

A lot of pros are sponsored. This means they get money in return for advertising a company at contests and winning them. Most pros earn around US$ 400 per contest won.

Martin Cernik (Czech Republic) performing a backside 360 at the 2002 Winter X Games.

Winter X Games

These are held in one of the big American resorts in January each year. The Winter X Games hold competitions for skiing, snowboarding, snowmobiling and snowskating.

THE OLYMPICS

Snowboarding is growing in popularity at the Olympic Games.

Disciplines

Today, snowboarders compete in half pipe, parallel giant slalom (a race) and snowboard cross – an exciting race with jumps, banks and other obstacles.

Men and women compete separately.

Men's parallel giant slalom, Winter Olympics 2006

52

SNOWBOARDING

Men's snowboard cross competition, Winter Olympics 2006

Olympic snowboarding first appeared at the 1998 Winter Olympics in Nagano, Japan, with giant slalom and half pipe events.

At that time, the resort of Nagano still hadn't opened its lift to regular snowboarders!

Men's snowboard cross competition, Winter Olympics 2006

BIG AIR

Every few years someone comes along and breaks the height barrier – launching themselves highest in the air.

Ingemar's Air

Swedish snowboarder Ingemar Backman smashed the record for the world's highest quarter-pipe air in 1996. He was measured at 7.5 metres above the pipe.

Heikki 'The Flying' Sorsa

Finland's Heikki Sorsa recorded the highest-ever quarter-pipe air when he styled an amazing Method grab at the 2001 Arctic Challenge.

The air measured 9.5 metres.

Sorsa performing a Method grab.

Terje Håkonsen

Terje Håkonsen broke Sorsa's record at the Oakley Arctic Challenge in 2007.

Terje hit an incredible 9.8 metres in height – and performed a 360 at the same time!

MILESTONES

Who has played their part in setting some of the milestones in the history of snowboarding?

The largest drop from an aircraft on a snowboard was performed by USA's Mike Basich in 2003. He jumped out of a helicopter at around 34 metres.

SNOWBOARDING

Terje Håkonsen recently became the first known person to ride a wave on a snowboard. He was towed by a jet ski in Hossegor, France.

In 2001, Marco Siffredi became the first person to climb and ride down Mount Everest. In 2002 Marco attempted to ride down the steeper north face, but he disappeared and was never seen again.

The North Face, Mount Everest (8,850 metres)

Need for speed

The fastest snowboarder in the world is Australia's Darren Powell. In 2001 he rode his board at a scary 201.90km/h.

GREAT RIDERS

Jake Burton

In 1977, Jake started Burton Snowboards from a workshop on his farm in Vermont, USA.

Shaun White

American Shaun has won a gold medal in at least one international championship each year since 2003, including the 2006 Winter Olympics.

Craig Kelly

US pro Craig was the first freeriding professional. He was killed in 2003.

Terje Håkonsen

This Norwegian topped a 2004 poll as the most influential snowboarder on the planet. His name has been given to two snowboard tricks: the Håkonflip and the J-Tear.

Hannah Teter

Hannah Teter, Olympic gold winner in 2006, is a master of the half pipe. In 2002 she was the first woman to land a 900 in a half-pipe competition (aged 15).

Tom Sims

This snowboarding pioneer from the US was a keen skateboarder. In 1977 he started producing snowboards in his garage under the Sims name.

David Benedek

REAL-LIFE STORIES

" I can't believe how hard the first couple of days snowboarding were in the very beginning. I don't think anyone really gets a break from those, no matter how talented they turn out to be! **"**

David Benedek, Germany

❝I've had some really scary situations in Alaska ... we were hiking along the ridge with cornices on either side. It's really dangerous. The guy was about four metres in front of me, and I said, 'On the left here, there's a cornice,' and as he took one step to the side, the whole cornice just went. It wasn't humungous, but it was big. If he'd have gone, he'd ... maybe not have been killed, but he'd have been scared. And I think that was about as scared as I've been. **❞**

Terje Håkonsen, Norway

Terje Håkonsen

❝Snowboarding is fun to me because you get to travel all the time ... which I think is why I still do it so much. **❞**

Adam Gendle, UK

Adam Gendle

Glossary

Air The time a rider spends off the ground.

Cornice An overhanging of hardened snow at the edge of a mountain rock face or cliff.

Frontside and Backside This refers to which way the spin goes – left or right!

Half pipe Built with snow, a half pipe is a vertical U-shaped structure. Like a skateboarding half pipe, riders use the walls to get air and perform tricks.

Monoski A kind of forerunner to the snowboard. The rider stands on the middle of the board with their feet together facing forwards, and wiggles their hips to turn.

Nose and Tail The front (nose) and back (tail) of a snowboard.

Obstacles Half pipes, picnic benches, handrails – anything that you can snowboard on.

Powder Deep, newly fallen, fluffy snow. This is what all snowboarders want to ride in.

Skate parks Concrete and wooden parks for skateboarders. This idea was copied by snowboarders and they called them fun parks.

Skateboarding A popular urban sport that has influenced snowboarding.

Spins What most tricks are based on. Because riders are strapped to their boards, they cannot perform the same flips as skateboarders. So they jump and spin 360 degrees or more in the air.

Surfing The first board sport, from which skateboarding and snowboarding originated.

Thaw Occurs when snow melts as spring arrives. In Western Europe, this is usually at the end of April and beginning of May.

Toe edge/Heel edge The edges of a snowboard bordering on the toes/heels of the rider.

Wax Snowboarders apply wax to the base of their board to make sure it glides smoothly on the snow.

Index